10 EASY

without cutting your nose off:

DISCLAIMER: This book is for entertainment and informational purposes only
and the contents herein should be used at your discretion and best judgment. Nik
Scott is not a licensed/trained/practicing stylist, cosmetologist or beautician. Nik
Scott is not responsible or liable for adverse or undesirable affects including hair
loss, hair breakage or other hair/scalp/skin/body damage as a direct or indirect
result of the contents herein.

10 EASY STEPS TO GO NATURAL

without cutting your hair off!

NIK SCOTT

This book is dedicated to my loving husband and daughters. Thank you for inspiring me, motivating me and believing in me. I love you from here, past the moon!

Acknowledgements

ALL honor and glory, in everything I do, belongs to my Heavenly Father. It isn't me who authored this book, it is Him speaking through me! Thank you, God for the many giftings with which you have trusted me - both spiritual and natural!

to Richard: Thank you for your ongoing support, understanding, encouragement and outside of the box ideas! You complete me!

to J.A.S.: Thank you for showing me parts of myself that I never even knew existed! You truly are the best pieces of me!

Thank you **to every person who has ever** visited *Long Hair Don't Care*, watched my YouTube videos, liked my Facebook page, followed me on Twitter or supported LHDC-TV. I wouldn't have even thought to do this without you! *HUGS*

Table of Contents

Preface

When I started *Long Hair Don't Care* in October 2008, the natural hair movement for women with highly textured hair was in FULL swing! Natural hair blogs, forums and websites were popping up like heated kernels of corn, and every time I turned around, I found myself reading yet ANOTHER testimony about someone who did the big chop and how free they felt. More and more, I was seeing images of women donning their highly textured tresses in my personal life - commercials, catalogues, movies and even on mannequins in the mall!

I began to wonder what my own natural hair looked like. I kicked myself in the butt for falling victim to the contents of the relaxer jar three months earlier - AFTER going *a year and a half* without relaxing! Every time I saw a beautiful head of huge natural hair, I told myself,

> *"If I would've just hung in there for a few more months, my hair could look like that..."*

I regretted ending my transition. But the fact of the matter was, **I WASN'T READY**.

My first transition lasted from March 2007 until July 2008. I relaxed my hair again on January 3, 2009 and that was the last time a chemical called sodium/calcium hydroxide found its' way onto ~~the new growth~~ my natural hair. My second transition wasn't an attempt, it was a success! I cut the last of my relaxed ends on February 7, 2011.

My name is Nik and I've successfully gone natural, _without_ cutting all my hair off and it is the BEST thing I've ever done for my hair! In this book, I'm going to share with you 10 easy steps to go natural, my story as well as best practices to help you get started and complete your journey to natural hair without cutting your hair off!

Step One

YOU Have Options

If I had $5.00 for every time somebody told me,

"I wanna go natural, but I don't wanna cut all my hair off!."

I'd be a rich woman! One of the purposes of this book is to highlight that there's more than one way to go natural! Granted, the most popular and well known method of going natural is what's known as the big chop, or BC for short. The big chop is exactly what it sounds like - cutting off all your hair and basically starting from scratch. Some women choose to wait a month or two after their last relaxer touch-up before they BC, while others opt to whip out the clippers and shave their heads G.I. Jane style!

The big chop experience can vary greatly from person to person. I've heard testimonies about how liberating a big chop is. I've heard about the many changes and adjustments women go through after they BC. Some women feel less pretty with very short hair. Some women adorn themselves with cosmetics, accessories, dresses and heels to make themselves feel (and look) more feminine. Some women are so confident, comfortable and excited for their BC, they don't feel anything but euphoria!

Although I didn't go natural with a traditional BC, the benefits of going natural this way cannot be overlooked:

1. Your natural hair journey begins INSTANTLY

2. There's really no turning back...at least until your hair grows out

3. You have the opportunity to learn your natural hair immediately

Of course there are also drawbacks to big chopping as well, but most of them have to do with the statement I opened this chapter with; short hair, limited styling options, the potential stress one may feel going from hair one second to no hair the next. But the BC blues are really contingent upon how long or short your hair is before you big chop in the first place. I think it's pretty safe to say that the person who rocks the short Halle Berry is likely to have a less shocking big chop experience than the person who has hair down her back and decides to big chop - but either way a BC ain't for everybody...and that's O.K.!

STEP ONE:

*Decide how you want to go natural. You can either big chop or transition. Both methods have pros and cons but you have to decide which one is right for you, your hair and your lifestyle. **YOU** have options!*

The second way to go natural, is to do what I did, and that's transition to natural. Going natural by transitioning is nothing more than growing out your

---

relaxer. Many people do not believe this is an option for them because of the way they've been trained by their stylists. Although this mind set is gradually changing, many stylists still warn their clients not to go too long between relaxer touch-ups because their hair will break off. This word of caution is true, but not really. I will go into more detail about the stylist's word of caution in Step 3.

A transition is a real and viable option to go natural that more and more women are choosing every day! What transitioning allows you to do is slowly go natural, without cutting all your hair off at once. The benefits of transitioning are many, including but not limited to:

1. You can ultimately go natural when you're good and ready

2. You can grow your natural hair to a length that you're comfortable with before you cut the relaxer out

3. You have a wide variety of styling options

And just like there are drawbacks to BCing, there are drawbacks to transitioning and I will help you get through them the best I can in the proceeding pages in this book.

Step Two

A Piece Of Cake

I have one failed transition under my belt, not because I didn't WANT to go natural, but because I wasn't READY to go natural. I entered my first transition prepared for all of the physical changes that were going to take place. I was ready for the overflow of ~~new growth~~ natural hair that I had, I was even prepared for styling changes that I needed to do. What I wasn't prepared for was the mental transition going natural took me through, and my mind eventually took over the matter.

I'm a mother and I always tell my girls,

"Things are what you say they are."

But I should add to that,

"Things are what you THINK they are!"

The more ~~new growth~~ natural hair I had the more frustrated I became with my hair. As prepared as I thought I was for styling changes, I wasn't. I resorted to wearing my hair in a bun all the time. ALL.THE.TIME! I didn't know what else to do with my hair. The more ~~new growth~~ natural hair I had, the longer wash day took. I went from a 10-15 minute detangling session on wash day to a 45-60 minute session. I was going through products like crazy and the reason(s) I opted to go natural were slowly, but steadily being buried under every new centimeter of ~~new growth~~ natural hair that grew out of my scalp. I dreaded doing my hair. I never felt like being bothered with it. I found myself thinking only negative thoughts about my hair. I didn't like the way it looked, I didn't like the way it felt and I didn't like wearing that dog'on bun every day! Then, one day, all of that negative energy I was emitting into the atmosphere about my hair, came back to me. I couldn't take it anymore! I went to my local drug store, bought a home relaxer kit and that was all she wrote. In less than the time it took to detangle my hair, my year-and-a-half long transition was over.

STEP TWO:

Think of every step of your transitioning process as sweet. Remove the sour thoughts from your mind as soon as they start to creep in. Stay focused on the reasons why you wanted to go natural in the first place. This is a process, much like the process it takes to get to a piece of cake.

AND IT FELT **GOOD**! To see my hair hanging past my shoulders in a way I hadn't seen in over a year was so refreshing! The 10 minutes it took me to comb out my hair almost had me convinced that it was all worth going back to the only thing I knew. Little did I know, the very last time I would go through the process of basing, gloving, mixing, timing and neutralizing was only six months into the future.

If you're like me, your hair has been relaxed for as long as you can remember. If you're like me, you have no idea what your natural hair looks like without processed ends hanging off of it. If you're like me, you never even considered going back natural until the natural hair movement was in full swing. If you're like me, you are motivated and inspired by all of the beautiful heads of luscious natural hair you see on a daily basis. And if you're like me, you're starting your journey back to your hair's roots excited and nervous at the same time

Transitioning to natural hair is a process and like any other process, it seems to get worse before it gets better. Think about the process of baking a box cake. Cake mix, eggs, oil and water when packaged individually don't seem too bad, right? Before you begin the process, the ingredients are nice and neat and easy to handle. However, in order to get to that tasty slice of cake, you have to put the cake mix into a bowl, crack your eggs over it, dump oil and water on it and mix it all together. If you scooped up a handful of your cake at this point, it wouldn't be so easy to handle or control. You'd have batter seeping between your fingers dripping, everywhere but where you want it! In fact, your cake is worse off than it was before you started! BUT THE ***PROCESS*** ISN'T OVER! You still have to pour your cake into prepared pans, bake it, cool it and frost it. Even though the cake is sweet during every step of the process, it isn't until the entire process is complete that you can finally sit down and enjoy a piece of cake with a cool glass of milk or a scoop of your favorite ice cream.

Think of your transitioning process like the process of making a cake. Before you get started your hair is neatly packaged and easy to handle. Right in the midst of your transition your hair will seem to be uncontrollable, but once your process is over, you can sit back and enjoy the delicious fruits of going natural!

Step Three

True Or False

So, you wanna go natural without cutting your hair off, huh? Well, you have to pass the transitioner's entrance exam first! That's right, you have to become an expert on the common truths and falsehoods about natural hair BEFORE you can become a certified, card-carrying member of the transitioner's club! From great-grandmothers to grandmothers to mothers to daughters, misinformation about natural hair has been passed down for generations - *you don't have good hair, natural hair doesn't grow, natural hair can take a lot of abuse, you have to cut off all your hair to go natural* - and more times than not, what you've probably heard all your life about natural hair isn't exactly true, and what's worse, most of it is NEGATIVE.

Remember: Things are what you <u>THINK</u> they are!

So, if you think you don't have good hair or natural hair doesn't grow or you have to cut off all your hair to go natural, guess what? THAT'S WHAT IT IS! I've already discussed how important it is to maintain positive thoughts during the transitioning process, so I will just get to the questions and answers to the test.

Everyone will be as excited as you are about your decision to go natural.

FALSE

One would think that as popular as going natural has become, it would be a widely accepted practice, but the truth is, it isn't. Natural hair is still viewed by many as unprofessional, unkept and unacceptable. Your decision to go natural won't be received well by everyone and sometimes it won't even be received well by those closest to you. If going natural is something that you *truly* want to do, you will have to figure out how to encourage yourself sometimes. There are great support groups online, and there may even be regular natural hair meet ups in your area. Do your best to surround yourself around people who support your decision and don't let the naysayers get into your head.

You have to cut off all your hair to go natural.

FALSE

This has been a common thought for who knows how long! For decades, our stylists have told us that if we go too long between relaxer touch-ups our hair will

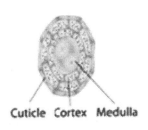

Cuticle Cortex Medulla

break off or shed excessively. This word of caution is true, but not really. What your stylist knows that you probably don't is how a relaxer alters the structure of your hair. Without getting too boring and scientific, your hair is made up of three layers, the cuticle, the cortex and the medulla. The cuticle is your hair's protective layer and the cortex is where temporary alterations - like moisturizing and roller setting - and permanent alterations - like chemical processing, take place. In other words, for a relaxer to work on your hair, the cuticle must be damaged or completely removed (remember this is the protective layer) in order for the chemical to reach the hair's cortex and make the permanent change. Excessive heat usage can work the same way, damaging/removing the cuticle and permanently altering the cortex. Have you ever seen someone with curly hair straighten it and go back curly only to notice their hair wasn't as curly as it was before they straightened it?

> **SIDE NOTE:** *Temporary hair alterations, such as roller sets, work similarly, but instead of damaging or completely removing the cuticle, the cuticle is temporarily lifted allowing whatever product to reach the cortex, thus encouraging your hair to temporarily take on the shape of the roller.*

Now that I got that technical stuff out the way, let's get back to the stylist's word of caution and how it's true but not really. In a nutshell, when your ~~new growth~~ natural hair comes in, it is unaltered and your hair's protective layer is pretty much in tact. That ~~new growth~~ natural hair is therefore stronger than the previously relaxed hair. The point at which your ~~new growth~~ natural hair meets the relaxed hair is the weakest point on your hair's strand and extremely susceptible to breakage - this is where your stylist is right. However, this breakage can be significantly reduced with gentle handling and proper moisturizing techniques which will be discussed more in Step 7. So, YES, there will be breakage during a transition to natural hair. Will you go bald? NO! And with gentle hair care practices, going natural without cutting your hair off becomes a reality.

Natural hair is healthier than processed hair.

TRUEish

Healthy hair...now, that's a term that's thrown around a lot, but the truth is, hair can't be healthy or unhealthy. Why? Because once hair grows out of your scalp it's dead, and something that's dead can't be healthy or unhealthy. So, your next question might be, then why do people say it? Well, I can't know for sure, why people refer to hair as healthy or unhealthy, but my best educated guess is this term is used to describe the way hair looks, feels and reacts. When you think of healthy hair that way, it's simple to conclude that natural hair is healthier than chemically processed hair. The cuticle layer in processed hair has been, at best, compromised, and this leaves the rest of the hair vulnerable. While the cuticle layer in unaltered natural hair is primarily in tact leaving the rest of the hair protected. This means your hair is able to retain moisture better.

Moisturized hair feels soft and supple. Moisture also enhances elasticity when it comes to hair. The more elastic your hair is, the longer it takes to break. Think of a rubber band. A rubber band can stretch a long way before it breaks. Elasticity in your hair works very similar to that. An in tact cuticle layer also means that your hair will be shinier and stronger.

I don't have good hair. I can't go natural.

FALSE

I literally cringe when I hear someone refer to hair as good. BUT. I know where they're coming from. When people refer to hair as good they're talking about the kind of hair they perceive as tame, manageable and not too kinky. The statement and perception of good hair is divisive, negative and downright rude, in my opinion. Again, your hair IS what you think it is, so if you think your hair is good, no matter what texture it is, guess what? YOUR HAIR **IS** GOOD period If you have hair on your head, guess what? **YOU** have good hair. Do you know how many women have lost their hair due to health and/or environmental factors? I'll bet these women would gladly take your kinky-curly-coily-knotty-frizzy-cottony hair in a heart beat! You know why? Because **YOUR HAIR IS GOOD**! So since your hair is good, guess what? YOU can go natural.

Your natural hair will be just like the texture of your new growth.

FALSE

While you're transitioning your new growth can give you a general idea of what your natural hair will be like. The more new growth you have, the more of an idea you get. However, you will not truly know what your natural hair looks like until all relaxed ends are gone. See, the relaxed ends of your hair kinda weigh your new growth down making it appear to be more stretched than it will be once your transitioning process is over. Oftentimes, the moment you cut the last of your relaxed hair off of your new growth, your natural hair will spring into place, shrinking half its stretched length or more!

STEP THREE:

Distinguish between what's true and untrue about natural hair. Recognize some of what you have believed your whole life may not be true. Some of what your stylist tells you may not be true. Going natural is not only a process of the hair, but a process of the mind.

Natural hair doesn't grow.

FALSE

Hair growth is not dependent on gender, texture, presence/absence of chemicals or race. Unless there are certain environmental and/or health hindrances, the average growth rate for human hair is 1/2" per month. That's AVERAGE not guaranteed. Some people's hair grows slower than 1/2" per month and some people's hair grows faster than that. Natural hair often appears to "not grow" because of the nature of it. Highly textured hair in its natural state is generally tightly coiled and zig-zaggy. It can stretch fifty percent or more in length! I like to compare natural hair to a spring, because of the springy like quality it has. This springy quality means that it could take a whole lotta growth before your hair will start to hang and look long. Natural hair has a tendency to grow out before it grows down - but that doesn't mean your hair's not growing. If length is something you're concerned about, check your growth progress from time to time by stretching your hair to see where it hangs.

Natural hair is harder to take care of.

FALSE

Will your natural hair require more time? Most likely yes, but more time doesn't mean harder. The fact of the matter is, most women don't spend the time they should in taking care of their hair whether it's natural or not.

My hair is natural, now I can be rough with it.

FALSE

This is a very common misconception. Because of its tightly-curly/zig-zaggy structure, the cuticle in natural hair is literally, tightly-curly/zig-zaggy and that means there are sections on your hair's strand that aren't as protected as other sections. The unique nature of the cuticle in natural hair means that it is weak. The more kinky/zig-zaggy your hair is, the weaker it is and because of this, rough combing, brushing and styling are a no-no.

Step Four

Do You Really Want It?

Natural hair. Do you really want it? If you've truly made up your mind that you want to go natural without cutting your hair off, you're going to have to take some time and figure out what is it that you REALLY want. Okay, you want to go natural and you want to do it by transitioning. But WHY do you want to go natural? Do you want to go natural because you miss your natural hair after being relaxed for a short period in your life? Do you want to go natural because you've suffered repeated damage to your skin and/or scalp from chemical burns? Do you want to go natural because you want to see if your hair falls into those beautiful curls you see on the head of your favorite YouTube vlogger? Do you want to go natural because everyone else seems like they're doing it? Do you want to go natural because you want to set an example for your daughters? Do you want to go natural because...

There are a host of reasons as to why you would want to go natural, you just have to figure out what that reason is for you and fall back on that reason when you find yourself discouraged during your transition.

DO YOU REALLY WANT IT?! You've determined your reasoning for wanting to go natural, and you've determined that you want to go natural by transitioning rather than by big chopping. Now you need to determine how long you want to transition for. Transitioning to natural can be broken down into two subcategories, short-term and long-term. A short-term transition is growing out your relaxer for 6-12 months before cutting your processed ends and a long-term transition is growing out your relaxer for 12 months or longer. Remember that human hair grows an average of 1/2" per month, so theoretically, the longer you transition, the longer your stretched natural hair will be when you finally rid your hair of altered ends. But also remember, that you WILL have to cut the processed ends off at some point. They will not just disappear.

STEP FOUR:

Now that you know you really want it, figure out your reason(s) for going natural. Determine how long you will transition and understand that permanently altered hair is caused by chemicals and heat.

Natural hair. Yes, NATURAL hair, do you really want it? If you really do, then figure out what natural means to you. Clearly, natural hair is hair that isn't chemically processed to permanently change the texture of your hair. But what about hair where the texture is permanently altered by heat? Remember the brief science lesson I gave you in Step 3? A simple way to define natural hair is:

***hair that, when soaked with water, returns to the
state in which it grows out of your scalp***

If at any point in your natural hair journey, you
realize that your hair, in part or in whole, doesn't
return back to the state which it grew out of your
scalp, you aren't natural. In order to "get your hair
back" you will either have to big chop or transition
again.

If you plan to wear your natural hair straight
the majority of the time, you will need to take
precautions when styling your hair to ensure that you
don't end up with permanently straight hair as a result
of excessive heat. Low tension blow drying
techniques, regular deep conditioning treatments, heat
protectant sprays, lotions and serums and running the
flat iron over your hair as few times as possible are all
ways you can reduce the chances of damaging your
hair's structure with heat.

Step Five

The Changes
I'm Going Through

L ike your hair, change is GOOD, but it isn't always simple, comfortable or even likable! As you begin your transition to natural hair, you're going to immediately take notice of the changes that your hair is going through! You're going to notice that your hair seems to be shedding more. You're going to notice that your hair seems to crave more moisture. You're even going to notice that, the more ~~new growth~~ natural hair you get the shorter your hair looks! But don't fret, these are all very normal changes, in fact, I like to categorize the changes of a long-term transition into three phases.

PHASE I: New Growth

Phase I of the transitioning process begins the day you decide you want to transition and ends somewhere around six months into your transition. The new growth phase is probably going to be the easiest phase for you to get through because most

SIDE NOTE: *The length of this phase is highly dependent on how often you received relaxer touch ups. If you received your relaxer every three months and never waited six months between relaxers, your new growth phase would end sometime around the four or five month mark and month six would actually begin Phase II of your transition. It is key to pay attention to your hair in order to accurately determine what phase of the transitioning process your hair is in.*

people have already entered this phase at one time or another while their hair was relaxed. When your hair is relaxed you have to do a touch up every so often to match your ~~new growth~~ natural hair with the rest of your hair, right? Well, sometimes that touch up happened at a later date than normal so you probably got pretty good at hiding the new growth until you were able to get your touch up.

PHASE II: Protective Styling

Protective styling is putting your hair in any style where the ends of your hair are tucked away and not exposed. Types of protective styles are buns, braid extensions, wigs or French twists. Months six through twelve mark the protective styling phase of the transitioning process. This phase is generally the most difficult. During this phase you will begin to experience an abundance of ~~new growth~~ natural hair, and you might not know what to do with it! Your wash day is going to start taking longer at this point and you will probably begin to have second thoughts about completing your transition to natural. Many people opt to big chop, get braid extensions, wigs or sew-in hair extensions during this time frame because taking care of their hair AND the two distinct textures is JUST TOO MUCH!

During this phase you will also begin to notice that your hair seems drier than normal and you may find more hair in the teeth of the comb on wash day.

This is normal. Remember back in Step 3 we talked about the point on your hair's strand where your ~~new growth~~ natural hair meets the relaxed hair being the weakest? Well, since you've probably never had this much ~~new growth~~ natural hair before, you most likely aren't taking the time you need to detangle or moisturize your hair. During this phase you will need to start detangling your hair in sections and grow used to the fact that those 10 minute detangling sessions are over. You are going to have to take your time when detangling in order to reduce the amount of breakage. There are several products available to help with detangling. Many detangling products are specifically formulated to eliminate knots and tangles while adding conditioning benefits as well. These products help your hair become manageable and make your detangling process simpler. Invest in a good detangling product and use it when you comb out your hair. Further, begin implementing a solid moisturizing routine. I will talk more about moisturizing in Step 7.

Understand that Phase II is just a part of the overall process! Keep your eye on the sweet fruit that is your 100% natural hair and lean on the reason(s) that you want to go natural. You will make it through!

PHASE III: Blending

This phase lasts from twelve months on, and for most people this phase goes off without much of the strife of Phase II. During Phase III you are beginning to have so much ~~new growth~~ natural hair that even protective styles aren't working so you look for alternative styling methods to deal with your hair. A lot of people go for what they know best during this phase (and sometimes even before they get to this phase) and that's heat styling. Heat styling can be very risky while transitioning to natural. It is very common for people to use excessive tension and heat in order to blend their ~~new growth~~ natural hair with the relaxed ends. Excessive heat and tension can cause highly textured to become permanently altered from what its natural curl pattern is. The problem likely won't be evident while you're transitioning, but once your process is complete, and your hair is 100% natural, you will be able to better see any difference in curl pattern between the roots and ends of your hair. And if you find that there are any differences, and you truly want natural hair, you'll have to transition again, but this time to rid your hair of heat altered ends instead of chemically altered ends.

"Does that mean I can't use heat during my transition?"

No. My advice is always get through your transition the best way you can, but keep heat usage to a minimum, just in case.

Instead of heat styling during Phase III, opt for hair styles that are more reminiscent of natural hair. During this phase in my transition, I relied on a "curly cheat fro." I achieved this style by putting my freshly washed hair in 15-20 braids or twists, rolling each section up on a 1/4" soft twist roller, allowing the set to dry completely and then taking it all down.

STEP FIVE:

Like your mind, your hair is going to go through many, MANY changes! Become familiar with the phases of the transitioning process and develop a plan to help you best get through them. Avoid relying on hairstyles that prevent you from learning & becoming familiar with your natural hair texture.

This style worked great for me up until the day I cut off the last of my relaxed ends. Other styles that work great for blending are twist sets, braid sets, roller sets, straw sets and even corn rows.

You hair will go through many changes while you're going natural. Your best offense will be a great defense. Go into your transition with an open mind, an open heart and a proactive approach. Get familiar with the phases of transitioning and keep in mind that the best time to get to know and experiment with your natural hair isn't when you're fully natural, it's while you're transitioning! Limit your reliance on long-term hair styles (like braid extensions, sew-in hair extensions or heat) so that you can begin to learn your natural hair.

Step Six

Treat It
Like It Wants To Be Treated

Have you noticed, just about every time the words new growth have been written in this book, they've been crossed out and replaced with the words NATURAL HAIR? I didn't do that for the ease of editing. I did it because the moment you make up your mind that you want to go natural without cutting your hair off, you have to stop thinking of the hair growing out of your scalp as new growth and start thinking of it as natural hair.

Clearly, the purpose of this book is to give you 10 easy steps to go natural without cutting your hair off. I mean, that's one of the reasons you bought this book, right? You want to go natural (for whatever reason) but you don't want to have to cut all your hair off to do it. I've already discussed the process of big chopping to go natural in Step 1. I briefly outlined a few of the pros and cons of the big chop in that chapter as well. What I didn't mention is that when you big chop, there is little to no time to transition your thinking, in terms of your hair, from new growth to natural hair. The moment your big chop is complete, your hair is natural and there is no room for interpretation.

However, when you transition to natural, the journey to natural hair is a gradual one. At the start of your transition you have much more relaxed hair than you do ~~new growth~~ natural hair so it may be difficult for you - or anyone else - to look at your hair as natural at that point. As your transition continues, your ~~new growth~~ natural hair will begin to overtake your processed ends, but because you still have relaxed ends, your hair isn't "truly" natural. So, again, it's difficult at this point to look at your hair as completely natural. But the problem with looking at your hair as new growth as opposed to natural hair isn't a visual matter, it is an emotional and psychological matter.

STEP SIX:

The moment you make up your mind that you want to go natural without cutting your hair off, you must start thinking of, and treating your hair in the state in which you ultimately want it. This isn't just a visual transitioning journey, it's an emotional and psychological one as well.

I cannot stress enough how important it is to retrain your mind during your transitioning process to natural hair. This book is meant to inspire, help and encourage you during your journey. This book is also designed to equip you for your journey. Your hair is going to go through many changes that are easy to understand and grasp because you can SEE the changes. You can TOUCH the changes. Other people can see and touch those changes as well. So the visual changes you will go through are very easy to identify. The emotional and mental changes you will go through are not so easy for you to see, or identify. My purpose for replacing the words new

---

growth with the words NATURAL HAIR is a deliberate strategy that hopefully speaks to your subconscious about your ultimate goal. Your ultimate goal is natural hair, not new growth. That's the way you should begin to treat your hair.

During your transition you will find that your ~~new growth~~ natural hair seems drier than your processed ends. Your gut reaction will tell you to take care of the hair that is represented the most on your head. At the start of your transition you will have more relaxed hair than ~~new growth~~ natural hair and toward the end of your transition, you will have much more ~~new growth~~ natural hair than relaxed hair. Regardless of what phase you are in during the transitioning process, you should treat your hair as if it is fully natural. So, if you feel your ~~new growth~~ natural hair is craving moisture, step up your moisturizing and deep conditioning routine. Don't concern yourself too much with the look and feel of your processed hair as all of that hair will eventually be cut off. From the very beginning concern yourself, instead, with the look and feel of your ~~new growth~~ natural hair as that will be the hair that you are left with when your transitioning process is complete.

Step Seven

The 3C's

Perhaps one of the most intimidating parts about going natural is figuring out exactly what you're going to do with your hair! *How* are you going to take care of it? If going natural really IS a healthier option for your hair, what can you do to ensure that your hair is being all it can be?

There really are no guaranteed answers to those questions, however, you can certainly make sure you are taking proactive hair care measures by building a solid natural hair care routine. Now I can't tell you what products to use or even how often you should be washing or conditioning your hair...you'll have to take the time it takes to get acquainted with your hair by paying close attention to it and observing how it reacts to certain products and/or processes. What I CAN tell you are the foundational building blocks of a natural hair care routine and those are the 3C's - CLEANSE, CONDITION & CARE!

As a new natural, you will need to figure out what products work and what products don't work for your hair. There really is no other way to truly figure that out except by trying new products. Sometimes it helps to get recommendations from others, but keep in mind that recommendations are just that. Don't expect to use a recommended product on your hair and get the same results as the person who recommended it. Your natural hair is like your finger print - no one (not even your mother, sister or daughter) has hair like yours. Your natural hair is unique to YOU and **_no one_** has the same hair as you.

As a guide, the new natural's shopping list should include a cleansing agent, deep conditioner, water-based moisturizer, seamless wide-tooth comb, soft boars-hair bristle brush, plastic conditioning caps, satin pillow cases/scarves/bonnet and a natural oil. Now this list is by no means exhaustive, but it's a great starting point for building up the 3C's.

CLEANSE

The first step to building a solid natural hair care routine is figuring out how you are going to cleanse your hair. That is, determining how you're going wash your hair and how often. Forget about the advice that you may have been given that natural hair will dry out and break off if it is washed too frequently. Well, let me take that back; there is some truth to that statement depending on WHAT you are washing your hair with...but remember, that WATER is the best moisturizer for your hair and natural hair craves and thrives on it.

There are several ways that you can cleanse your hair and scalp including traditional shampoo, Ayurvedic powders, oil washes, apple cider vinegar mixes or plain ol' conditioner, just to rattle off a few. As a new natural, ask yourself:

"How am I going to cleanse my hair/scalp?"

If you choose shampoo as your cleansing method, try to use shampoos that are free of sulfates and harsh detergents and always dilute your shampoo with 3 parts water to 1 part shampoo. When used frequently, sulfates can be very drying to natural hair and using them too often can make your scalp itchy, cause split ends, compromise your hair's cuticle and even cause breakage. When you shampoo, try focusing on getting your scalp clean, rather than the length of your hair. When you rinse, the shampoo run-off should be sufficient to clean your hair without stripping your hair of necessary oils and moisture.

Many women with highly textured hair (including myself) have found the best method of cleansing is to use conditioner. Many consumer brand conditioners are formulated with surfactants and, unless your hair/scalp are extremely dirty or built up with product, these surfactants are enough to cleanse your hair. Be mindful, though that an occasional shampoo cleansing will be necessary. Just pay attention to your hair and if it begins to feel waxy or stiff, use shampoo to cleanse rather than conditioner.

CONDITION

The conditioning step in the 3C's specifically refers to deep conditioning. Deep conditioning with a moisture-based deep conditioner is a great practice to incorporate into your natural hair care routine. Deep conditioning revitalizes natural oils, hydrates and

---

protects your natural hair. ~~Your deep conditioning treatment can be done on wet or dry hair~~, with or without a dryer/heating cap. ~~Conditioners formulated for deep conditioning are ideal, but not necessary~~. Many have had ~~great results using a regular conditioner for deep conditioning~~...but, again, you will have to experiment and find out what works best for your hair.

A deep conditioning treatment is different than a regular rinse out conditioning treatment. In a deep conditioning treatment, the product is typically left on the hair for ~~15-20 minutes~~ and then rinsed out, while in a rinse out conditioning treatment, product is applied to the hair and rinsed out after about 5 minutes. There is no right or wrong way to deep condition, however the quickest way to deep condition is under a hooded or bonnet dryer, heating cap, etc. If you choose to use external heating sources (such as a hooded/bonnet dryer or heating cap), your hair isn't being deep conditioned the first 10 minutes because it takes at least that long for the cuticles of your hair to open up - *and open cuticles are what makes this process different from simply rinsing out the conditioner after a wash.* Once the cuticles are open, it is easier for the conditioning product to reach the depths of your hair, resulting in better conditioned, strengthened and moisturized hair.

An alternate method of deep conditioning is by ~~doing the process overnight~~ and allowing your body heat to open your hair's cuticles. This process takes longer but sometimes is more convenient. Many find deep conditioning on wet hair after cleansing is best, but some prefer to deep condition on dry hair PRIOR to cleansing. You'll have to experiment and determine which method works best for you, your hair and your lifestyle.

CARE

Care is the most involved step in the 3C's because anything outside of cleansing and conditioning, falls under the umbrella of care. Care includes what kind of moisturizer are you going to use? What kind of comb and/or brush are you going to use? How often are you going to comb and/or brush your hair? How often are you going to use direct heat? How are you going to style your hair on a daily basis? What about trims? What kind of oil will you use? How will you cover your hair at night????

Caring for your natural hair is where most people get trapped. There are just so many questions that need to be answered and no real way to get direct answers! The best way to sort out the caring part of your hair care routine is to take it one step at time. If you find that a process within the care part of your routine isn't working for you, stop doing it and try something else.

MOISTURIZING

Because of the zig-zaggy, curly structure of textured hair, the natural oils that your body produces (called sebum) cannot reach the ends of your hair. This is why highly textured hair is drier than wavy or straight hair. Natural hair CRAVES and THRIVES on moisture and because you cannot rely on sebum to moisturize *you* must replenish the moisture in your hair.

> **SIDE NOTE:**
>
> OIL AND GREASE ARE NOT MOISTURIZERS!!!
>
> *In order for an oil or grease to truly moisturize your hair, the molecular structure of it must be small enough to penetrate past the cuticle in order to reach your hair's cortex. Only the molecules of coconut, olive and avocado oils are small enough to do this. All other oils simply sit on top of your hair.*

As mentioned previously, WATER is really the BEST and ONLY moisturizer your natural hair needs. If simply using water isn't going to cut it for you, there are several good moisturizers on the market. While shopping for your moisturizer, look for products that have water listed as one of the first three ingredients. How many times should you moisturize? There really is no magic number. I tend to moisturize my hair when it feels dry or when I notice my hair seems less elastic, and for me that's usually about every three days. You will have to find out what that timeframe is for you.

COMBING/BRUSHING

Combing and/or brushing is otherwise known as manipulation. The more you manipulate your natural hair the more prone to breakage it is. Reducing and minimizing breakage is essential if you are at all interested in retaining length and seeing hair growth. In general, the less you manipulate your natural hair, the less it breaks and the more growth you will see! Even if you aren't concerned with how long your natural gets, breakage is never good so try to limit the amount of time you spend manipulating your hair with combs and brushes. A practice that I've been following for years is to only manipulate my hair with combs/brushes on wash day, and that really seems to work for me.

When you detangle your natural hair, do so on wet hair, drenched with conditioner and only use a seamless, wide-tooth comb, detangling in sections. Work through knots, mats and tangles with your fingers and NEVER rip through them.

If you're like me and must use a brush from time to time, invest in a soft boar's bristle brush; really that is all you need to smooth down your edges. Or, for a less expensive option, use a soft bristle toothbrush instead.

DIRECT HEAT

Direct heat is the type of heat that you put directly on your hair - like blow drying, flat ironing, pressing and hot curling. Frequent use of direct heat not only compromises the integrity and structure of your natural hair texture, but if not used properly, direct heat can literally burn the ends of your hair off. Plus, direct heat is drying to natural hair, making it more prone to breakage. Is there ever a time when direct heat is necessary? Absolutely! I love straight hair! But rather than using direct heat as a crutch to "deal" with your natural hair, use it as a treat!

STEP SEVEN:

Just as important as the 3C's is being consistent with your natural hair. Realize that what works for some may not work for you. Do what's best for YOU, YOUR hair and YOUR life style. Make a commitment to your natural hair. Remember this is a PROCESS and the longer you stick to it and take the time to understand and figure it out, the prettier and tastier the end results will be!

Prior to using direct heat, give yourself a protein treatment - that is using a protein-based conditioner following the manufacturer's instructions - followed up by a deep conditioning treatment and when you detangle, use your favorite heat protecting spray, lotion or serum. All of these steps will help protect the integrity and structure of your natural hair texture.

✗ **BEWARE!** NO preventative measure is 100% and natural hair is: *hair, that when soaked with water, returns to the state in which it grows out of your scalp.*

STYLING

Natural hair is SO versatile! You can braid it, twist it, set it, roll it, curl it, pic it, bun it, pony tail it, puff it, loc it...or just wear it in its natural state! How you choose to wear your natural hair is up to you. I have found that low manipulation hair styles (like twist sets or braid sets - *setting my wet hair in twists or braids and then taking it down*) work best for me, but others have found that simply wearing their hair in a wash-n-go works, while many love to keep their hair twisted, loc'd or braided! You will have to get in your hair and experiment with different styles to find what works best for you, your hair and your lifestyle.

TRIMMING

Basically, unless your natural hair is damaged (breakage or excessive split ends) it is not necessary to set a trimming schedule. However, in my personal experience, I find that regular trimming helps keep my hair not only looking better, but stronger as well. The ends are the oldest and most fragile part of your hair and keeping them "young" and vibrant helps them to be stronger and more resilient to daily wear and tear. So do you HAVE to trim your hair? No, not at all! Trimming is all a matter of preference.

AT NIGHT

Cover your natural hair each night with either a satin scarf or bonnet. This simple practice will help to preserve your hairstyle and help to preserve the moisture levels in your hair. Use satin as opposed to cotton because cotton is highly absorbent and will rob your hair of precious moisture. Satin is less absorbent. If you do not want to cover your hair, sleep on a satin pillow case instead - but note that covering your hair is most effective.

The 3C's are not the be all end all to building a natural hair care routine. You will have to be consistent with whatever you choose to do and commit yourself to your natural hair journey. Fall back on the reason(s) you wanted to go natural and flood your mind with positive affirmations! There is no one way to care for natural hair. Do what's best for you, your hair and your lifestyle even if it seems different than what everyone else is doing.

Step Eight

Get Scissor Happy

Dictionary.com defines the word transition as:

"movement, passage, or change from one position, state, stage, subject, etc., to another; change: the transition from adolescence to adulthood."

The whole point of transitioning to natural is to CHANGE your hair from one state to another. The only way that the change from relaxed hair to natural hair can occur is by cutting your hair. You can grow your relaxer out for 5 years, but if you never cut the relaxed portions of your hair, the change has not completely taken place - *you are still in transition*. Now, let me clarify. The title of this book specifically says that I will give you 10 easy steps to go natural without cutting your hair *off* - NOT go natural *without cutting your hair...*

The change that takes place in your hair when extreme heat or chemical processes are applied is permanent. There is no way, chemically or otherwise, to get your hair back to the state it was, without cutting the permanently altered parts out of your hair.

While transitioning from relaxed hair to natural hair your focus should be on the parts of your hair that are natural not the parts that aren't. Develop a hair cutting schedule and stick to it. How much or how little you cut is up to you, the important thing is for you to be consistently working toward your goal

---

of natural hair and one of the best ways to do that is to cut the relaxed hair as your natural hair grows out.

Some of you may be thinking,

"I love the length my hair is now!" **or** *"I don't want to cut it!"* **or** *"I'm so close to my next length goal and if I cut it, I'll be set back!"*

STEP EIGHT:

Get scissor happy! Choose a target date that you will be fully natural and make your last cut. The only way to reach your ultimate goal of natural hair is to CUT the relaxed ends off of your hair. Set up a consistent cutting schedule and cut the relaxed ends as your natural hair grows out.

To those of you who hold these sentiments and other feelings like it, my advice is:

During your transition, focus only on one goal at a time.

If there are length goals that you are seeking, it really defeats the purpose of transitioning because you will have to cut your hair. If you're seeking the goal of natural hair, it defeats the purpose of having length goals because you HAVE to cut your hair! You will need to figure out what is most important to you, is it length or is it natural hair?

"So, now you're telling me that I can't have long hair AND natural hair!"

NO! I'm not saying that at all! One of the great things about transitioning to natural hair instead of big chopping is once your transition is complete, you have a little length to your hair. Again, your focus while transitioning should be on the parts of your hair that are natural. Rather than holding on to and falling

---

SIDE NOTE: *The closer your ~~new growth~~ natural texture is to your relaxed texture, the "smoother" your transition may be in terms of breakage. The more different your ~~new growth~~ natural hair is from your relaxed hair, the more prone to breakage it is. Regardless of the texture your ~~new growth~~ natural hair appears to be, treat your hair gently. If you find that you just can't seem to get the breakage under control, AND you're committed to going natural, don't be afraid to cut your transition short and big chop.*

---

in love with the length of your hair in total, begin to redirect your length goals toward the natural hair that is growing out of your scalp.

Now that's enough talk about length, let's get back to going natural! I've already touched on the importance of setting up a regular cutting schedule. The next thing you need to determine is how long you're going to transition for. If you decide that you will transition for two years, pick a date around that time and make your final chop! Don't beat yourself up if you don't make it to that date. Most people (including myself) don't transition as long as they had initially planned, and that's O.K. You may wake up one day during your 20th month of transitioning and decide it's time. You may go longer than your target date, and that's O.K. too! Do your final chop when **<u>YOU</u>** are ready!

Step Nine

I Wanna Know What Love Is: P.R.D.E.

L ove is patient. Love is kind. The way that you deal with your hair should be in love. The thoughts you have about your natural hair should be those of love. Patience. Kindness. Love. But all of that is easier said than done - ESPECIALLY while you're transitioning!

Transitioning from relaxed to natural hair should be an exciting chapter in your life but the fact of the matter is, many women begin this journey with mixed emotions, with apprehensions, with doubts. Many women don't know HOW to love their hair, let alone how to deal with it in a loving manner - whether it's relaxed OR natural! Loving your hair is actually easier than you may think and it goes beyond the surface of "accepting natural hair." Here, I'm going to outline a few basic steps to help you LOVE your natural hair so that you CAN start to be patient with it and treat it with kindness.

P

Develop a sense of **pride about your natural hair**. It really is difficult to love something that you aren't proud of. About 15 months into my transition I uncovered what pride about my hair meant for me. It donned on me that no other group of people has hair like mine. It occurred to me that the qualities of kinky-curly hair are specific ONLY to those who are blessed with such hair. The fact that NO other group of people on the planet has hair like this made me smile. I felt a warmness come over me. It motivated me to want to finish out my transition!

Think about what it is that makes you proud about your natural hair. What are those things that make you excited when you think about ultimately being natural? Dig deeper than the reasons you chose to go natural and seek something that is just as unique as your hair will be!

STEP NINE:

*Learn how to love your natural hair using **P.R.D.E.** as a foundation. Figure out what **P**ride in your hair means for you, **R**espect your natural hair and the transitioning process, **D**on't give up & **E**mbrace what <u>YOU</u> got!*

R

R-E-S-P-E-C-T your natural hair! It's hard to love something that you don't have respect for! Yes, I get it. Your hair isn't a person...or *IS it*? Natural hair tends to have a personality that's very different than its owner. A person who is introverted and calm may have natural hair that's wild and crazy! This transitioning process is more than about going natural. It is about relinquishing control. It's about respecting the process so in the end you can respect your highly textured hair for everything it IS and everything it DOES!

D

Don't give up! It's not easy to love something that you've given up on. Even after you've made up your mind, even after you've surrounded yourself with loads of support and even after you've transitioned for 8 months, there will likely be a time when you simply feel you can't go on! There will likely be a time when thoughts of relaxing creep back into your head. There likely will be a time that you wonder WHY you're even doing this...but HANG ON!! The majority of women who have completed their transition will tell you it was well worth it! I, for one, have no hesitation in telling you that going natural is the BEST thing I could've done for my hair and I WISH I would've done it long before I did! Not the product search, nor the transitioning frustrations, not even the time it takes to do my hair, make me want to go back relaxed. The fact of the matter is, in most cases, if you ever want to wear your hair straight the majority of the time, you DON'T have to be relaxed to do it!

E

    Embrace what <u>YOU</u> got. If you don't even like it, it's pretty darn hard to love it, ain't it? But curl envy is REAL! Comparing your hair and the qualities it has (or doesn't have) to other people's hair is a common practice but it isn't the best practice. There will be so many qualities that you secretly wish your hair had, or things that you secretly wish your hair could do, or you may even secretly wish your hair looked like hers, but guess what? YOUR hair doesn't have *those* qualities or do *that* thing or *look like hers* and you have to just come to grips with that. Embrace the qualities that **YOUR** hair has and the things that **YOUR** hair does and the way **YOUR** hair looks! Now there's nothing wrong with admiring other heads of hair. In fact, admiration is a good thing as it frequently leads to inspiration! Just don't let that admiration leave you comparing your hair to someone else's - remember, *<u>your</u>* hair is GOOD ☺

Step Ten

Whip Your
{Natural} Hair

Y OU DID IT! You've successfully made it through your transitioning process and you couldn't be HAPPIER! You didn't let the matter take over your mind. You've learned how to love and respect your natural hair! You've even developed a solid hair care routine!

NOW WHAT????

Well, NOW the _fun_ part begins! You will have to spend some time getting acquainted with your hair now that it is without relaxed ends. Your hair will not behave the same as it did while you were transitioning. The styles you put it in won't be as predictable as they used to be. In fact, as a natural, you may not even be able to rely on the same styling options you did when you were transitioning. I encourage you not to get frustrated. I encourage you to fall back on the reasons you wanted to go natural. Recall that P.R.D.E. you have about your natural hair!

I remember the day I did my final chop. I remember how EXCITED I was to finally be natural! After all, THIS was a goal that I was striving for for the past two years of my life! I immediately put my hair in twists for a twist set. But when I took them out, I was sorely disappointed with the way my hair looked. The only thing I knew to do after that was to put my hair into two-strand twists. And I STILL didn't like it! As excited as I was to be natural, I felt that my hair was short. Even after transitioning my natural hair to a length I thought was good, my hair was SO short to me! This lead me to experiment with tons of styles! After about two weeks, I didn't even realize how "short" my hair was and I rolled on with my natural hair journey as happy as a clam!

STEP TEN:

Even after your transition is over and you're finally enjoying the sweet fruit of natural hair, stay focused and stay positive! Experiment with styles and accept your hair for what it wants to do! And by golly, don't forget to WHIP YOUR {NATURAL} HAIR!!! *YOU deserve it!*

I remember the day I did my final chop. I remember how EXCITED I was to be natural! After all, THIS was a goal that I had been striving for for the past two years! I was so excited I took camera phone pictures of my hair and messaged everyone I knew! But you know what? They didn't even realize that I had cut my hair. They didn't even NOTICE the difference between my transitioning hair and my natural hair! I was stunned by those reactions because my hair seemed so "short" to me!

Perception will always be reality and the perception you have about your natural hair will be your reality. Was my hair short when I big chopped? That all depends on what your definition of short is. My hair was long enough to pull back, twist up, puff out and even set on rollers...but yet *I* felt it was short...

      After your transitioning process is complete, don't place limitations on your natural hair! Your new hair is probably unlike any other hair you've dealt with on your head. Jump right in and start experimenting with styles and accept your hair for what it wants to do when it is in these styles. If your hair doesn't fall into perfect coils or soft ringlets, THAT'S OKAY! If you find that your natural hair always has sort of a frizz to it - EMBRACE IT! Even if your natural hair shrinks 80% of it's stretched length, LOVE YOUR HAIR!!! Your hair is GOOD and NO ONE has hair like YOU! Maintain that same positivity you had while transitioning and WHIP YOUR {**NATURAL**} HAIR!

Appendix

EVERYTHING YOU NEED TO KNOW ABOUT SCAB HAIR

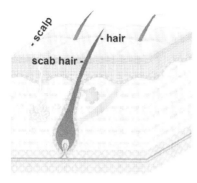

What is scab hair? Scab hair the hair directly beneath the scalp that has been adversely affected by chemical processes such as hair relaxing and dying. When this hair emerges from your scalp as new growth, it is often rough, dry and very brittle. Scab hair is NOT your true texture as it has been "treated" with chemicals and is typically a bit straighter than your true natural hair texture. When transitioning, it can take up to 6 months before the true texture of your hair emerges depending on how long you were chemically processed, what type of chemical(s) you used and the strength of said chemical(s).

Why is all that important? Many new transitioners are overwhelmed with the excitement of their new journey and are very anxious to discover (or rediscover) what their natural hair texture is like. Scab hair is NOT your true texture. Many new transitioners can become discouraged after a few months when they find the new growth they have is not what they thought it would be. As with many things in life, transitioning gets better with time!

Well, I've been transitioning for 3 months, and my hair is not like that. Am I abnormal? No. Not everyone is affected by scab hair. It is primarily dependent on how long you were chemically processed, what type of chemical(s) you used and the strength of said chemical(s).

Can anything be done to prevent it? Not really. The hair beneath your scalp, if damaged, is irreversible. However, the best thing you can do to help reduce the dryness and brittleness of scab hair is use aloe vera on your scalp. Known for it's healing properties, aloe vera will penetrate your scalp, help repair your follicles and moisturize the hair directly beneath your scalp. Maintain a consistent moisturizing hair routine including moisturizing deep conditioning treatments and using a water-based moisturizer. Like chemicals, the only thing that will completely remove scab hair is a good pair of scissors.

TRANSITIONING HAIR & SCALP ELIXIR

This recipe is great for relieving itchy dry scalp that often comes with transitioning to natural. These ingredients have healing properties and will help soothe your scalp, soften and moisturize your hair.

- 1-1/2 oz aloe vera juice
- 1/2 oz liquid MSM (methylsulfonylmethane)
- 1/2 oz steeped chamomile
- 1 drop rosemary essential oil
- 1/8 teaspoon liquid vitamin E oil

DIRECTIONS: Mix all ingredients together and put it in an applicator bottle. Massage into your scalp and new growth as needed. Moisturize and style as usual. Store in a cool dry place and use within 48 hours.

*All ingredients can be found at your local health food and/or vitamin store.

TRANSITIONING HAIRSTYLE INSPIRATION

Transitioning to natural hair is one of the most exciting chapters in your life and it shouldn't be painful when it comes to figuring out how to style your hair. As you read in Step 2, one of the reasons that I failed my first transition was because I was bored with my hair style. I didn't think I had any other options as a transitioner. Well, my second transition opened my eyes to a whole new world when it came to styling my hair! I discovered that a bun wasn't my only option, but a LAST resort! Use the next few pages of this book for inspiration and know that you don't have to wait until you are natural to start enjoying the versatility of your hair!

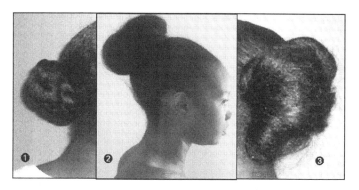

THE BUN or **CHIGNON** *for the fancy folks!*

Buns are among the simplest and versatile styles you can wear while transitioning. You can wear a high bun, a low bun or a bun to the side. You can braid it, twist it, roll it, tuck it under or just do the donut.

1. For the first bun, the hair was freshly washed, conditioned and detangled. The hair was then put into a low ponytail, and divided into two sections. Each section was then put into a large two-strand twist and then twisted the around each other. The style was finished by pinning the ends of the twists into place.

2. Bun number two was created on blow dried hair. The hair was placed into a very high ponytail. Next, the ponytail was fanned out by finding the center of it and flattening it out. Starting in the back, the hair was rolled under, and around to create a donut effect. The style was finished by pinning the ends into place.

3. The last bun was styled on flat ironed hair.
Starting with a low ponytail, the hair was separated
into two sections but instead of two-strand twisting
the sections, the sections were twisted around
themselves. The bun was finished by wrapping the
two sections in opposite directions and securing the
ends with hair pins.

TIP! To give your buns and ponytails a sleek
smooth look, after styling - spritz your edges with a
bit of water, brush them down with a soft bristle
brush and then tie on a satin scarf. Leave the scarf on
for about 20 minutes and then take it off.

INDIVIDUAL TWO-STRAND TWISTS

Individual two-strand twists are a popular hairstyle among women with natural hair, but you don't have to wait until you are fully natural to start wearing them!

To achieve this style, start with freshly washed, conditioned and detangled hair. Starting at the nape, pinch about a 1/2" section of hair and clip the rest of the hair out of the way. Begin twisting the hair from the top using the tighten and twist technique - that is ensuring the twists are good and taut as you twist down to the ends of the hair. Continue to twist in 1/2" sections until all of the hair is twisted.

SOFT ROLLER WAVES

This is a fun hairstyle that is typically done on relaxed hair, but who says you can't do it on transitioning hair! This style is simple to achieve and gives a different look.

After blow drying the hair, roll it on extra large rollers in 2" sections starting from the back. When rolling the hair, start at the TOP, instead of the ends. With one hand, hold the roller close to your head and wrap the hair around the roller with your other hand.

Steam rollers were used for this look, but you can easily achieve this style with non-heated rollers by setting the hair and leaving the rollers in for several hours before taking them out.

FLAT IRON

In my opinion, there is NOTHING like freshly flat ironed hair! There really is no replacement for it. If you decide to use direct heat on your transitioning hair, be sure to take note of the tips in Step 7 and understand that NO preventative measure is 100%.

The hair was freshly washed, conditioned, detangled and blow dried. Starting at the back, the hair was parted in 1/2" sections and a flat iron was used to straighten until all the hair was done.

THE CURLY CHEAT FRO

This was my signature hairstyle while transitioning. This style allowed me to truly get acquainted with my hair and kinda get used to big hair....it made me feel like I was natural. This style is great because of its versatility and how well it blends the ~~new growth~~ natural hair with the relaxed ends.

1. This is the basic cheat fro. The hair was freshly washed, conditioned and detangled. The wet hair was braided into about 15-21 plats. The entire length of each braid was rolled on a 3/8" soft twist roller. The set was dried completely before removing the rollers, unraveling the braids and fluffing the hair.

2. This is a different angle of the basic cheat fro pictured in style #1.

3. This is a variation of the basic cheat fro. The curls were smoothed to one side and pined down with large bobby pins. Water, a soft bristle brush and a satin scarf were used to achieve a sleek, smooth finish.

4. Again, this is the basic cheat fro, BUT instead of using 3/8" inch rollers, a larger size roller was used and the hair was parted on the side.

5. The fifth look was achieved by braiding the hair in larger braids and setting each braid on larger rollers.

TIP! To preserve the curly cheat fro, the curls were simply tucked under a satin bonnet before bed. In the morning, all that needed to be done was shake and go!

HOW TO CUT RELAXED ENDS

The purpose of transitioning is to ultimately have 100% natural hair. Regardless of how much or how little relaxed ends you have remaining at the end of your transition, the way you will cut your hair will be the same. Your final chop can be done by someone you trust, or you can do it yourself!

You will need:

Sharp hair cutting shears

Conditioner

A comb

Large mirror

- Before you begin cutting your hair you will have to identify the point at which your relaxed ends meet your ~~new growth~~ natural hair. Many successful transitioners have found it is easier to see this point when the hair is wet and loaded with conditioner.

- Divide your hair into four sections. Starting in the back, part 2" sections and begin cutting your hair

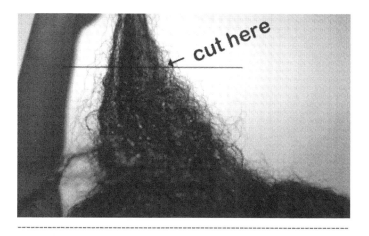

right at the point where the ~~new growth~~ natural hair meets the relaxed ends. You will want to do this in front of a mirror in a well lit room.

- Continue cutting 2" sections of hair until all relaxed ends are gone.

The final cut!

hair before

hair after

THINGS TO REMEMBER:

✔ Upon cutting the relaxed ends off, your hair will likely shrink, making it appear shorter than it's stretched length. That's O.K.! The springy-like quality of highly textured hair is one of the many things that makes it unique!

✔ The ends of your hair will be very blunt after your chop. Allow your new natural hair to "get used to itself" for a about eight weeks before you begin to shape it and cut it further.

✔ It is very common for there to be relaxed ends that were missed during the cutting process. Take some time examining your hair over the next few weeks and snip any remaining relaxed ends.

✔ Your new natural hair is probably unlike any other hair you've ever had on your head, and THAT'S what makes it so exciting! Start your new journey with an open mind and experiment with different hair styles. You've been striving for this a long time so have fun!

HOW TO CHOOSE A STYLIST

In the world of do-it-yourself haircare, gone are the days of getting your hair fried, dyed and laid to the side. BUT while you're on your transitioning journey, and even once you become natural, there *may* just come a time that you want to get your hair done. Now, you may have a stylist that's been doing your hair since you were two, but for those who don't, or if you don't have access to your regular stylist, you'll have to go through the grueling process of finding a stylist who you TRUST with your hair. There really is no easy way to find out if you trust a stylist except to let him or her actually do your hair. But before the two of you even get to such an intimate point, you, as the stylee, can go through a simple 3-step process before you hand over your precious tresses to someone who can undo months of progress in less than point oh-two seconds.

STEP ONE *Identify A Reputable & Recommended Stylist*

Perhaps the most daunting part of finding a hairstylist is the process of trying to figure out WHO to go to! At this point in your process, you're probably happy with your progress and you certainly don't want anyone up in your head telling you what you're doing is wrong or worse, completely undoing all the good that you've been so diligent about doing with your hair.

The first place you should look is to your family and friends for suggestions. Ask people you trust and find out who they recommend.

If your family and friends are of no help in your quest, stop a stranger whose hair you admire and ask her. MOST of the time the person you're asking will be very flattered and more than willing to share her stylist's information, if she has one.

The last place you can look (and probably the simplest, but most risky) is the Internet. There are many online beauty and hair resources that can help you find a hairstylist. If at all possible, look for online reviews about the potential stylist to help you make your decision.

STEP TWO *Drop By*

Once you've accumulated a list of about 3-5 potential stylists, **DO NOT** PICK UP THE

PHONE!!! This is not the time to start making phone calls. Even if the recommendation came from someone you know and trust, it is still heavily suggested that you do not omit this step.

Take some time out of your Saturday to drop by the salons where these potential stylists work. You'll want it to be on a Saturday because this is typically the busiest day for salons/stylists and you want to get a good feel of what the shop is like - *even when it's busy*. While you are at the salon, take a look around and take some mental notes - but make sure you are not being obvious. Look to see how many people are waiting - you don't want to spend your whole day up in the shop...take note of what kind of hair appliances and products are being used. Speak to one of the stylists and ask her/him some questions about pricing - at this point you don't want to ask specific questions, just be very general as if you hadn't planned to drop by - you really just want to get a good idea of what the atmosphere of the shop/stylist is like.

STEP THREE *Schedule A Consultation*

Just like Step 2, this step should never be omitted from the process of finding a hairstylist. Hopefully your list of stylists has dwindled some after you've dropped by the salons. If not, that's ok. You'll just have a few more phone calls to make.

Call up each stylist on your list and schedule an initial consultation. Make sure the stylist knows that this is not a visit to get services rendered, but a consultation visit. Most professionals in the hair styling industry do not mind sitting down with potential clients prior to the first time doing their hair. The consultation should be FREE of charge.

An initial consultation will do two primary things:

1. Allow you to know more about the stylist and
2. Allow the stylist to know more about you and your expectations for your hair

The consultation shouldn't take more than about 15 minutes. During this time you will want to ask the stylist a series of questions including:

*   How long have you been practicing/licensed?
*   What kind of products do you use?
*   Is it ok if I bring my own products for you to use?
*   What is your method of detangling hair?
*   What styling tools and appliances do you use?
*   What is your philosophy on trimming?
*   Do you charge extra for deep conditioning?
*   I'm transitioning to natural, how will you handle my hair?
*   What is your preferred method of styling natural/transitioning hair?

- How do you feel about heat training natural hair?
- How many natural clients do you have?
- What are the most popular natural hairstyles your clients request?

Note: this list of questions is not exhaustive and if you feel you need to ask additional questions please do. You'll want to make sure that the stylist you hire will be close to being as gentle as you are with your hair and ALWAYS ask for references.

During the consultation, wear your hair in an accessible style that will allow the stylist to feel and touch your hair and scalp. Let her/him know what your expectations are concerning your hair; how you like your hair to be handled, how hot you like your appliances, how many times you like your hair lathered. Find out if it's ok to bring your own products, etc.

Some Things To Remember...

• Don't start looking for a stylist a week before you want to get your hair done. Allow plenty of time to get through this 3-step process.

• IT'S YOUR HAIR! If at any time during your styling visit you feel uncomfortable or are unhappy with what's being done, let your stylist know. If letting them know does not work, leave. Yes,

LEAVE. Pay for the services that have been rendered and go on your merry way. This may seem like an extreme gesture, but the process to go natural is serious business and just because you're sitting in a stylist's chair does not mean you are at the mercy of the stylist. It's your hair and your money.

• Never, ever, EVER get a "trim" on your first visit! The first time your new stylist does your hair is not the best time for you to find out how scissor happy they are or aren't. Go to them a few times before you let them perform any type of heat services or cut your hair.

• Finally, understand that no one is going to be as loving to your hair as you. Enjoy your visit to the salon. It's supposed to be a pampering experience. Sit back, relax and savor the moment...

Q/A SESSION

Q. My hair is SO dry! What do you suggest?

A. I get this question a LOT. Many things can cause your hair to be dry such as genetics, environmental factors, health factors, products & food to name a few. You will ultimately have to identify the foundational cause of what's causing your hair to be dry. While figuring out what the cause is, you can begin to make small changes to your haircare routine. The first thing you should do is incorporate weekly deep conditioning treatments. Next, moisturize your hair with water or a water-based moisturizer on a more frequent basis. Finally, be sure you are consuming the recommended daily water intake for your body weight. *To find out how much water you should be drinking, divide your weight in half...for example, if you weigh 150 pounds you should be drinking at least 75 ounces of water each day.*

Find out more about developing your haircare routine, including deep conditioning and moisturizing in Step 7.

Q. What is a TWA?

A. The term TWA is often used when talking about a traditional big chop experience. TWA is an acronym meaning Teeny Weeny Afro.

Find out more about the big chop in Step 1.

Q. What is shrinkage?

A. Shrinkage is the amount, or lack of curl each hair strand has which causes your hair to appear shorter, or shrunken, when dry.

Find out more about shrinkage in step 3.

Q. I got my hair flat-ironed and I noticed my coils aren't as coily as before! What can I do?

A. Your coils may be suffering from a mild form of heat damage. Heat damage occurs when extreme heat and tension are applied to your hair - usually when blow-drying, hot combing and/or flat-ironing. Because the process of straightening textured hair requires that the cortex of your hair become temporarily altered, using heated appliances on your hair causes protein reduction in your hair. You can try using a protein-based conditioning product to replenish the protein loss in your hair. However, if there are strands of completely straight hair after flat-ironing, the coil may not come back at all.

Find out more about heat damage and preventions in Steps 3, 4, 5, 7 and 8.

Q. Do I need to trim my hair?

A. If you are currently transitioning, yes you will have to trim your hair. The only way to rid your hair of the relaxer is to cut it. If you are 100% natural, trimming is up to you.

Find out more about trimming and cutting in Steps 7 and 8.

Q. I wanna go natural but this all seems so intense and time consuming! Isn't there some kind of product I can use to reverse my relaxed hair back to natural?

A. No. The process of relaxing causes permanent changes in the chemical and bonding structures of your hair. The only way to rid your hair of relaxer is to cut it out either by big chopping or transitioning.

Find out more about the relaxing process in Steps 3 and 8.

Q. What is a co-wash?

A. Co-wash is a shortened term for conditioner wash. A conditioner wash is a widely used method of cleansing highly textured hair because it helps to preserve moisture levels in the hair.

To find out more about co-washing, see Step 3.

Q. I'm considering a Brazilian blow-out (keratin treatment). Should I get it?

A. Personally, I don't know much about keratin treatments, but from what I understand the process involves a high level of keratin, extreme temperatures of heat and lots tension. I cannot tell you what to do with your hair, but this is a process that I wouldn't take my hair through. If you want a straight look, consider flat-ironing and using the prevention methods discussed in Steps 3, 4, 5, 7, and 8.

Q. What is a stretched hairstyle?

A. Stretching refers to a hairstyle that reduces the amount of shrinkage the hair has when it's dry. Braid sets and twist sets are common stretched hairstyles.

See Steps 5 and 7 for more about braid and twist sets.

Q. What is a hair type? Why is it important?

A. Hair typing is a system developed by Oprah Winfrey's hairstylist, Andre Walker. Walker's hair typing system ranges from Type 1 to 4 and classifies the hair based on how much or how little curl it has, with Type 1 hair having no curl and Type 4 having the most...

In my opinion, hair typing has become more confusing than helpful because in order to accurately determine someone's "hair type" you would not only need to SEE the curl/coil of their hair, but you would need to touch their hair and observe how their hair responds to styling processes and products also. However, many new naturals find hair typing to be helpful. When looking for products many seek women with the same hair type as them with hopes that a particular product will work the same in their own hair.

Q. My transition is OVER! YAY ME! But can I use the same products now that my hair is natural?

A. Absolutely! My recommendation is that you continue to use the products you used while transitioning and don't get caught up in trying new things YET. Take a few weeks to get comfortable with your new natural hair before you begin the process of finding product staples. Being newly natural is overwhelming enough when it comes to styling and developing a routine without the added task of trying new products.

Find out more about choosing products in Step 7.

Q. I heard wearing a fro is bad for natural hair because it causes really bad tangles, breakage and dry hair. Is that true?

A. Part of embracing your highly textured hair is accepting your hair for EVERYTHING it can do! If you want to wear a fro, wear it! Wearing one is no different than wearing any other hairstyle. Take proper precautions when forming the fro. Here are a few tips:

• Pic/comb your hair into shape while it's wet and with a creamy leave-in conditioner. Apply your moisturizing products at this point.

• When your hair is about 80% dry, use your pic to further lift your hair at the root. Do not take the pic through the entire length of your hair, only lift the first 1-2 inches of hair.

• Use your fingers to shape and pic out the length of your hair until your fro looks the way you want it.

• To moisturize your fro use a water-based spritz daily and use your fingers to pic and work the product through.

• When it's time to wash your hair, use a spray bottle to wet your hair with water and apply your deep conditioner to your hair. Do this in sections. Deep condition your hair, and then proceed to cleansing your hair as you normally would.

22671397R00051

Made in the USA
Lexington, KY
09 May 2013